Catholic Book of Prayer for Children

By
REV. LAWRENCE G. LOVASIK, S.V.D.
Divine Word Missionary

Nihil Obstat: Rev. Msgr. James M. Cafone, M.A., S.T.D., Censor Librorum
Imprimatur: ✠ Most Rev. John J. Myers, J.C.D., D.D., Archbishop of Newark

The Nihil Obstat and Imprimatur are official declarations that a book or pamphlet is free of doctrinal or moral error. No implication is contained therein that those who have granted the Nihil Obstat and Imprimatur agree with the contents, opinions or statements expressed.

The Sign of the Cross

IN the name of the Father
and of the Son
and of the Holy Spirit.
Amen.

The Glory Be

GLORY be to the Father,
and to the Son,
and to the Holy Spirit.

As it was in the beginning, is now,
and ever shall be,
world without end. Amen.

Morning Offering

MY God, I thank You
   for giving me this new day.
I give You all my actions
   for the glory of Your Holy Trinity.

I offer You my whole life,
   my memory, my mind, and my whole
     will.

You have given them all to me;
   now I give them back to You.
Give me only Your love and Your grace.
With these I will be rich enough.

O Lord, guide my actions
   by the help of Your grace
   so that every word and work of mine
   may always be for Your honor
   and the salvation of my soul.

Holy Mother Mary,
   pray for me and protect me.
St. Joseph, keep me close
   to Jesus and Mary.

Prayer to My Guardian Angel

Angel of God,
my Guardian dear,
God's love for me
has sent you here.

Ever this day
be at my side,
to light and guard,
to rule and guide.

My dear Guardian Angel,
teach me to know God,
to love and serve Him
and save my soul.

Keep me from all danger,
and lead me to heaven.

The Our Father

OUR Father, Who art in heaven,
   hallowed be Thy name;
Thy kingdom come,
Thy will be done
on earth as it is in heaven.

Give us this day our daily bread,
   and forgive us our trespasses,
   as we forgive those who trespass
      against us;
   and lead us not into temptation,
   but deliver us from evil.
   Amen.

Prayer of Praise to the Lord

PRAISE God in His glory!
   Praise His power in heaven!
   Praise Him for the mighty things He has done!
   Praise His wisdom and greatness!

Praise Him with trumpets and harps!
   Praise Him with song and dancing!
   Praise Him with bells and music!
   Praise Him with joy and laughter!

Praise the Lord, all living creatures.

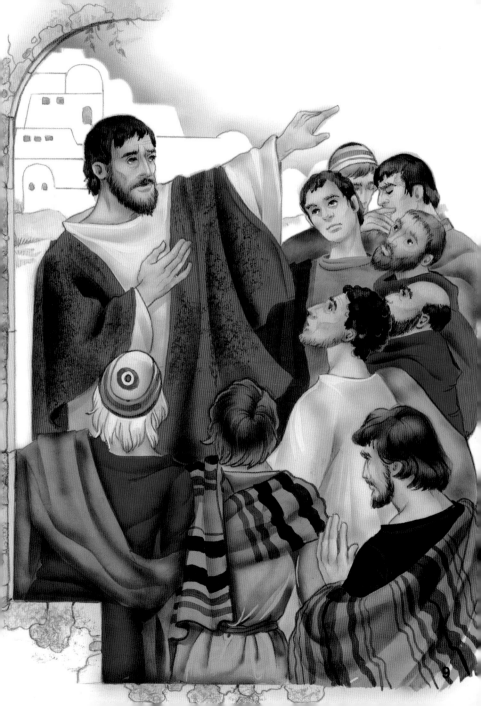

9

The Hail Mary

HAIL, Mary, full of grace!
The Lord is with thee;
blessed are thou among women,
and blessed is the fruit of thy womb,
Jesus.

Holy Mary, Mother of God,
pray for us sinners,
now and at the hour of our death.
Amen.

Offering to Mary

O MY Queen! O my Mother!
I give myself to you —
my body, my soul, and my whole
being.
Lead me to Jesus
and protect me from sin.
Keep me in your care
and take me to heaven.

The Apostles' Creed

I BELIEVE in God,
the Father Almighty,
Creator of heaven and earth,
and in Jesus Christ, His only Son, our Lord,
Who was conceived by the Holy Spirit,
born of the Virgin Mary,
suffered under Pontius Pilate,
was crucified, died and was buried;
He descended into hell;
on the third day He rose again from the dead;
He ascended into heaven,
and is seated at the right hand of God the Father
    Almighty;
from there He will come to judge the living and
    the dead.

I believe in the Holy Spirit,
the holy catholic Church,
the communion of Saints,
the forgiveness of sins,
the resurrection of the body,
and life everlasting.
Amen.

Act of Contrition

O MY God, I am heartily sorry
for having offended You.

I detest all my sins,
because of Your just punishment.

But most of all,
because they offend You, my God,
Who are all good
and deserving of all my love.

I firmly resolve,
with the help of Your grace,
to sin no more
and to avoid the near occasions of sin.
Amen.

Prayer for Mercy

GOD,
be merciful to me,
a sinner.

Act of Faith

MY God, I believe in You,
because You are the eternal truth.
Help me to accept Your word
and always remember
that You love me and care for me.
I believe in all that Your
Catholic Church teaches.

Act of Hope

MY God, I hope in You,
because in Jesus Christ, Your Son,
You have promised me Your love forever.
You will never leave me,
if only I stay away from sin
and remain with You.

Act of Love

O MY God, I love You,
because You are the Greatest Good
and deserve all my love,
as my Creator and my Father.
I love all people
because You want me to love them
for they are Your children too.

Prayer before Meals

BLESS us, O Lord,
  and these Your gifts,
which we are about to receive
  from Your goodness,
through Christ our Lord.
Amen.

Prayer after Meals

WE thank You, O God,
  for all these gifts,
which we have received from Your
  goodness,
through Christ our Lord.
Amen.

Prayer of Thanksgiving

GIVE thanks to the Lord,
  for He is good;
His kindness endures forever.

Prayer before
a Crucifix

LOOK down on me,
good and gentle Jesus,
while I kneel here.

Make my soul strong in
faith, hope and love.

Make me really sorry
for all my sins so I
will never sin again.

I am sad
when I see the wounds
on Your hands and feet,
and think of the words
of Your prophet, David:
"They have pierced my
hands and my feet."

Lord Jesus Crucified,
have mercy on us!

Hail, Holy Queen

HAIL, Holy Queen, Mother of Mercy;
   hail our life, our sweetness and our
   hope.

To you do we cry,
   poor banished children of Eve.

To you do we send up our sighs,
   mourning and weeping
   in this vale of tears.

Turn then, most gracious Advocate,
   your eyes of mercy toward us.

And after this, our exile,
   show unto us the blessed fruit
   of your womb, Jesus.

O clement, O loving,
   O sweet Virgin Mary.

The Prayer of Saint Francis

LORD, make me an instrument of
Your peace.
Where there is hatred, let me sow
love;
where there is injury, pardon;
where there is doubt, faith;
where there is despair, hope;
where there is darkness, light;
and where there is sadness, joy.

Grant that I may not so much seek
to be consoled as to console;
to be understood, as to understand,
to be loved as to love.

For it is in giving that we receive;
it is in pardoning that we are
pardoned,
and it is in dying that we are born
to eternal life.

The Memorare

REMEMBER,
   O most gracious Virgin Mary,
   that never was it known
   that anyone who fled to your protection,
   implored your help,
   or sought your intercession,
   was left unaided.

Inspired by this confidence,
   I fly to you,
   O Virgin of virgins, my Mother.

To you I come;
   before you I stand,
   sinful and sorrowful.

O Mother of the Word Incarnate,
   despise not my petitions,
   but in your mercy,
   hear and answer me.
   Amen.

Prayer for My Family

DEAR Jesus,
   I thank You for the good
mother and father
You gave me.

I thank You
   for my brothers and sisters,
   for my home,
   for my food and clothes,
   and for all the good things
   I receive.

Grant my parents grace and health
      on earth
   and a great reward in heaven.

Give our family peace and love,
   so that we may have
   a happy home.

Evening Prayers

MY GOD and Father,
   I thank You for
all the blessings
You have given me today.

I am sorry for all my sins,
   because they have hurt You,
   my dearest Father.

Forgive me, O God, and help me
   never to offend You again.

Have mercy on poor sinners
   and all who need Your help.

Bless my father and mother,
   my brothers, sisters and friends.

In Your name, O God,
   I go to sleep this night.

My dear Mother Mary,
   help me to love God more
   and keep me from every sin.

My Guardian Angel,
   help me.

Psalm 23: Prayer to the Lord, My Shepherd

L ORD, You are my shepherd;
   I have everything I need.
   You give me new strength;
   You guide me in the right way,
   as You have promised.

Even if that way goes through darkness,
   I will not be afraid, Lord,
   because You are with me!

Surely, Your goodness and love
   will be with me as long as I live.
   Your house will be my home forever.